I'M NOT WHO YOU'VE HEARD I AM

GEORGE BLOOMER

Unless otherwise indicated, all Scripture quotations are taken from the New King James Version of the Bible.

Copyright © 1998 by George Bloomer

Printed in the United States of America

All rights reserved. Written permission must be secured from the publisher to use or reproduce any part of this book, except for brief quotations in critical reviews or articles.

George Bloomer
P.O. Box 11563
Durham, NC 27703

ISBN # 1-892352-00-1

Dedication

This book is dedicated to Pastor Audley James of Revival Time Tabernacle in Toronto, Canada, who has proven to be a father in the gospel to me throughout my years of ministry and growth.

Acknowledgment

A special acknowledgment to my loving wife, Jeanie, for her continuous support.

CONTENTS

1   The Search For Truth 11

2   In the Midst of the Storm 17

3   Who Do You Say I Am? 23

4   Keys To the Kingdom 29

Foreword

If there's anyone who is qualified to write about how to discover who Jesus really is, it's Pastor George Bloomer! Over the years, Pastor Bloomer has written about a variety of timely topics, including *Warfare, Demons and How They Operate, Relationship,* and now this enlightening book on the Person of Jesus Christ. In this book, Christ will be communicated to you in a unique way as George Bloomer shares insight and revelation on a very important topic. The book is written in a style that is spiritual yet clear enough to introduce the reader to the true deity of Jesus, while at the same time developing one's understanding of the life of Jesus and the twelve disciples who traveled with Him.

Finally, the myths of who Jesus is can be permanently put to rest as Pastor Bloomer reveals the true Person of Jesus Christ through the uncompromised Word of God.

As Vice Presiding Bishop of P.A.W., I highly recommend this book. I believe you will view Christ in a different light after reading *I'm Not Who You've Heard I Am*.

Bishop Thomas Wesley Weeks Sr.

Introduction

Are you walking in the light of your freedom in Christ, or are you tripping over the cords of religious traditions and the doctrines of men? Although you desire to live in victory, are you exhausted from trying to weather the dark storms that come your way?

I've learned through my own personal experience that I can't depend on what someone else tells me about Jesus. I've discovered that the true identity of Christ can only come through prayer and personal and intimate fellowship with Him. And most of the time, this revelation knowledge comes in the midst of the storms in our lives—when the circumstances place us in positions where we must have divine intervention. The purpose of these storms are not to destroy us but to build our faith, perfect our character, and cause us to see who Jesus really is.

As you read this book, I pray that you will be enlightened and encouraged to know that you are not alone on your journey, and that Jesus is still at the helm of your ship in the midst of every storm. As you grow in your relationship with Christ, I believe you will learn to rest in every circumstance of life, knowing that in the storm, you will find His delivering hand.

...that I may know Him and the power of His resurrection...
—Philippians 3:10

1

The Search For Truth

Stand fast therefore in the liberty by which Christ has made us free, and do not be entangled again with a yoke of bondage (Galatians 5:1).

Many people today—including Christians — are going through life, accepting doctrines of men that have been passed down for generations. Others, in their search for truth regarding Jesus and His place in their lives, are easy targets for those who teach false doctrines of bondage and legalism. Because of their great hunger for something real in their lives, many are looking for a "quick fix." So they accept the theories of others instead of going to God and searching the Scriptures for themselves. And after a period of time, they begin to realize that not only is the teaching failing to satisfy their need—it is becoming a bondage to them.

This is legalism—a form of oppression that refers to the doctrines of "do's and don'ts." Early in my Christian experience, my initial impression of some Pentecostal denominations was that these were places of liberty and freedom—places where I could sanctify myself from all the worldly pleasures. Coming directly off the streets into the church, I had no problem submitting to the leadership of the pastor. I was excited to be walking in my new life. Finally I was drug free, and it felt good to be in the presence of people who showed genuine concern about me. For the first time I could remember, I was beginning to experience real peace and joy.

Then I was filled with the Holy Spirit. This, along with the Word of God, liberated me far beyond what my church was ready to receive. Not only was my newfound liberation in Christ less than acceptable to my church—to my surprise, they viewed it as outright rebellion.

Their views on some scriptures were very legalistic. For instance, 1 Timothy 4:7-8: *But reject profane and old wives' fables, and exercise yourself rather to godliness. For bodily exercise profits a little, but godliness is profitable for all things, having promise of the life that now is and of that which is to come.* In the church I attended, this scripture was interpreted to mean that Christians shouldn't play sports and should never be athletes.

For years, false doctrines of this nature stunted my spiritual growth because I wasn't receiving sound biblical teaching anywhere else. I have since learned that legalism is not the revelation truth of God. Instead, it is merely the opinions and doctrines of men. Anything taught in the Christian arena that cannot be backed with Scripture is not sound doctrine.

Unfortunately, some have strayed from teaching the truth of the Word of God and have slipped into the demonic doctrines of legalistic bondage. In order to be set free from the bondage of that kind of teaching, I had to search the Scriptures and gain knowledge of the Word for myself. No man had to lay hands on me in order for me to gain deliverance. It was simply the Word of God and the touch of the Holy Spirit that re-created me and set me free.

The Touch of Jesus

In Mark the eleventh chapter, there is an interesting account of Jesus sending the disciples off to get a donkey for Him to ride into Jerusalem. *"Go into the village opposite you; and as soon as you have entered it you will find a colt tied, on which no one has sat. Loose it and bring it. And if anyone says to you, 'Why are you doing this?' say, 'The Lord has need of it,' and immediately he will send it here"* (verses 2-3).

Jesus instructed the disciples to look for a specific colt, and He told them where to find it. He also made a point of saying it was an animal that had never been ridden. I think this is a significant point. If no man had ever sat on the donkey, it must have been an animal that had never been tamed. And if it had never been tamed, then it must have been WILD! Further investigation reveals that the donkey was tied up because undomesticated animals were not allowed to roam loose throughout the village.

In this account, we see both the power and the compassion of Jesus. Apparently there was no problem when Jesus approached the donkey to sit on it. This wild animal that had never been ridden was suddenly calm at the touch of Jesus.

Oh, can't you see that a lot of people have something in common with that animal. Many of us have had similar incidents at one time or another in our own lives. Many of us, before the touch of Jesus, went through a stage of lawlessness and rebellion...and we tasted the disappointment of being an outcast. Or maybe we allowed the opinions of other people to tie us down, causing us to live our lives in bondage. Because we were bound for so long, our growth was stunted and our ability to travel, investigate new ideas, and gain knowledge and insight was very limited. For anytime we walked too far, the rope of bondage would yank us and pull us right back to the place from which we began.

But when we realize that we're bound by the opinions and ideas of others and we begin to search for real truth for our lives, then Jesus touches us and makes himself real to us. And when Jesus touches us, we are suddenly different— we are a soul set free! Then we discover that He is the only true means of escape from the bondage and legalism of men.

Redeemed, But Not Storm-Free

In Isaiah 43:1-2, the Lord says, *"Fear not, for I have redeemed you; I have called you by your name; you are Mine. When you pass through the waters, I will be with you; and through the rivers, they shall not overflow you. When you walk through the fire, you shall not be burned, nor shall the flame scorch you. For I am the Lord your God"* (Isaiah 43:1-3).

You must realize that committing yourself to God does not insure that you will live a life that is free of storms and trials. Quite the opposite—this is often when the storms begin.

It is in the storm that we seem to feel alienated and cut off. Before God can move in your life, He must dismiss the crowd around you. As you stand isolated in the midst of the storm, God can make you and mold you into His divine image, giving you a better understanding of life and the important part He has in it.

2

In the Midst of the Storm

So he sent and had John beheaded in prison. And his head was brought on a platter and given to the girl, and she brought it to her mother. Then his disciples came and took away the body and buried it, and went and told Jesus.

When Jesus heard it, He departed from there by boat to a deserted place by Himself. But when the multitudes heard it, they followed Him on foot from the cities. And when Jesus went out He saw a great multitude; and He was moved with compassion for them, and healed their sick. When it was evening, His disciples came to Him, saying, "This is a deserted place, and the hour is already late. Send the multitudes away, that they may go into the villages and buy themselves food." But Jesus said to them, "They do not need to go away. You give them something to eat." And they said to Him, "We have here only five loaves and two fish." He said, "Bring them here to Me."

Then He commanded the multitudes to sit down on the grass. And He took the five loaves and the two fish, and looking up to heaven, He blessed and broke and gave the loaves to the disciples; and the disciples gave to the multitudes. So they all ate and were filled, and they took up twelve baskets full of the fragments that remained. Now those who had eaten were about five thousand men, besides women and children.

Immediately Jesus made His disciples get into the boat and go before Him to the other side, while He sent the multitudes away (Matthew 14:10-22).

Upon receiving the news of the death of John the Baptist, Jesus departed by ship only to find that a multitude was following Him—people who desperately needed a miracle from God. Because of their displeasure over the mass of people who were following Jesus after the death of John the Baptist, the disciples sought to send the people away. Nevertheless, the compassion of Jesus overrode the displeasure of the disciples, and He satisfied the need of the multitude by feeding them with only five loaves of bread and two little fish.

And when He had sent the multitudes away, He went up on a mountain by Himself to pray. And when evening had come, He was alone there (Matthew 14:23).

I see three important points in these verses:

1. Often, before Jesus can perform the miracle of building your faith, *He must separate you from the crowd.*

2. *Jesus went up to the mountain by himself to pray.* Jesus was always watching and praying. The mountain represents stability and heavenly places. So it isn't important whether you see Jesus or not. The important thing is to realize that *Jesus can always see you.*

3. *When evening came, Jesus was alone.* I can think of several interesting points about darkness. One is that Satan does some of his best work in darkness. Another is that the Bible sometimes uses the word *darkness* in reference to "ignorance" rather than "the absence of sunlight." So when we are alone in the darkness, we are very vulnerable,

and we must allow the Spirit of God to illuminate His Word to us, for Hosea 4:6 says, *"My people are destroyed for lack of knowledge."*

A Well-Known Storm

Let's examine a very well-known storm a little closer and see what its outcome has to reveal.

But the boat was now in the middle of the sea, tossed by the waves, for the wind was contrary (verse 24). The fact that the winds were contrary reveals that the ship had lost its direction. The ship represents our salvation and the contrary wind represents false doctrines.

Now in the fourth watch of the night Jesus went to them, walking on the sea (verse 25). The fourth watch represents the escape or deliverance. The fourth watch basically indicates the darkest hour. But this is of no relevance, for Jesus sees you from wherever He is.

And when the disciples saw Him walking on the sea, they were troubled, saying, "It is a ghost!" And they cried out for fear (verse 26). The disciples, fatigued from their long day of labor, were awakened by the winds wildly tossing their boat to and fro, only to see a form walking toward them on the water. Their abrupt awakening, coupled with the fierceness of the storm and the unusual sight they saw on the water, caused fear to strike their hearts.

Contrary winds can temporarily knock you out of fellowship with God and cause you to become alienated from the presence of God. But just when you are about to give up because of fear, Jesus comes to you and speaks a word of good cheer, as He did for the disciples in the next verse.

But immediately Jesus spoke to them, saying, "Be of good cheer! It is I; do not be afraid." And Peter answered Him and said, "Lord, if it is You, command me to come to You on the water" (verses 27-28). These verses speak of Peter's doubt. Although the fear was gone, Peter still had doubt.

So He said, "Come." And when Peter had come down out of the boat, he walked on the water to go to Jesus. But when he saw that the wind was boisterous, he was afraid; and beginning to sink he cried out, saying, "Lord, save me!" (verses 29-30). Finally, at the bidding of Jesus, faith was restored and doubt was abolished. In faith and obedience, Peter began to do the impossible—he began to walk on the water toward Jesus. But when Peter saw how strong the wind and waves were, fear again gripped him and he began to sink.

This is an important point you need to remember—*anytime you take your eyes off Jesus, your first step is down.* So when you step out on God's Word in faith, you must hold fast to it. You must never take your eyes off Jesus to look at life's circumstances, and you must never listen to any voice other than God's.

And immediately Jesus stretched out His hand and caught him, and said to him, "O you of little faith, why did you doubt?" And when they got into the boat, the wind ceased (verses 31-32). In the midst of Peter's fear and doubt, Jesus caught him. The sea represents life, and life always has its ups and downs. So anytime you launch out into the sea of life, you'd better make sure that Jesus is your anchor.

Then those who were in the boat came and worshiped Him, saying, "TRULY YOU ARE THE SON

OF GOD" (Matthew 14:33, emphasis mine). In the midst of the storm, the disciples sought the comfort and safety of the presence of Jesus...and they were not disappointed. They witnessed Peter walking on the stormy waters, and they watched in awe as Jesus caused the storm to cease. In the midst of their immediate and personal need, they discovered who Jesus really is.

The identity of Jesus was revealed to the disciples in the midst of a storm—a storm that was not seen at a distance, but a storm that encompassed them, consuming their self-confidence and self-reliance as men of the sea. It was in this storm that they began to look for deliverance. The deity of Jesus as the Christ was not revealed only through the many healings He performed, nor through His challenging sermons on the mountain. Oh yes, it was awe-inspiring to witness Jesus healing the leper and restoring sight to the man who had been blind from his mother's womb. But these miraculous, powerful, mind-boggling miracles did not reveal to the disciples, in a personal way, the true identity of Jesus. Revelation of who Jesus really is came in the midst of their own personal storm.

And so it is today. Jesus is not in the business of delivering you *out* of your storm. Instead He delivers you while you are *in* your storm, for it is in the midst of the storm that the true identity of Jesus is revealed. It is there that He allows you to see yourself for who you really are—but most importantly, it is where He reveals himself to you and lets you see what you can be with His help. *"With men it is impossible, but not with God; for with God all things are possible"* (Mark 10:27).

So, you see, the purpose of storms is not to destroy you, but to build your faith, perfect your character, and cause you to see who Jesus really is...in your own personal life.

3

Who Do You Say I Am?

"Who do men say that I, the Son of Man, am?" (Matthew 16:13).

In the sixteenth chapter of Matthew, Jesus put to rest any rumors that had been circulating among the crowds and the disciples as to His true identity. Notice in verse 13 that Jesus asked the ultimate question—but within His question, He told the disciples that he was the Son of Man. I believe this suggests that Jesus was looking for a more divine answer. So He encouraged them to give it some serious thought by saying, "Yes, I am the Son of Man—but who am I really?"

The disciples answered His question by repeating all the names that others called Him and believed Him to be. But Jesus wanted to know what *they* thought. So He got personal by asking His next question, *"But who do you say that I am?"* (Matthew 16:15).

These were men who walked with Jesus daily, witnessing the miracles He performed. Surely after worshipping Him and earlier declaring Him to be the Son of God, they all should have spoken up at once to reveal His identity. Nonetheless, this was not the case. Maybe the forwardness with which Jesus asked the question seemed a little intimidating for the disciples, but whatever the case, one voice finally spoke out.

And Simon Peter answered and said, "You are the Christ, the Son of the living God" (Matthew 16:16). Peter answered with assurance and boldness, giving a response that forever settled the question of who Jesus is. For as Jesus had previously stated, He was the Son of Man. However, the divine answer He was searching for flowed from the lips of Peter. For, most importantly, Jesus is the Christ, the Son of God. He is the Savior who came in the flesh as the Son of Man—but, divinely empowered, He is the Son of God and He is Lord.

Later in Matthew 16, Jesus began to reveal to the disciples some of the details about the events leading up to His coming death and resurrection. This information further confirmed in their minds that He was indeed the Son of God.

Jesus answered and said to him, "Blessed are you, Simon Bar-Jonah, for flesh and blood has not revealed this to you, but My Father who is in heaven. And I also say to you that you are Peter, and on this rock I will build My church, and the gates of Hades shall not prevail against it" (Matthew 16:17-18).

In this passage, Jesus not only confirmed Peter's answer but blessed him as well. Jesus knew that the Father had revealed himself to Peter because there was no way Peter could have reached this conclusion with his natural mind. No part of his intellect—and no amount of studying doctrine—could have given Peter this answer.

Such is still the case today. No amount of theological or doctrinal study can divinely reveal to us who Jesus really is. Studying the Word of God plants the seed, but it is the Holy Spirit who ultimately has to water this seed, causing us to grow and flourish into full revelation knowledge of who Christ is. This is also why the power of prayer is so important. It is during prayer that we "get a jump on things." During prayer we commune with God, and He reveals himself to us and gives us direction.

Old Things Are Passed Away

Therefore, if anyone is in Christ, he is a new creation; old things have passed away; behold, all things have become new (2 Corinthians 5:17).

When you accept Christ and receive the revelation of who He is in your life, you become a "new creation." And when Christ directs your steps, it's difficult to be led astray.

I know a young lady whose life is a great example of this. Before giving her life to Christ, this young woman sang for a very popular, award-winning pop group, even though she'd been reared in church as a young child. When she gave her life to Christ, she immediately resigned her secular singing career and dedicated her musical gift to the glory of God. But she was faced with tremendous pressure to return to her rock 'n' roll music career. The leader of the group couldn't believe she would give up a promising career in his group, and he pleaded with her to return, even offering to raise her salary. Eventually, other friends called to apply even more pressure to an already tempting offer. But she withstood the test and remained steadfast—refusing all offers, which seemed totally senseless to her old friends.

As time passed, the enemy soon applied more pressure by attacking her finances and her marriage. Although there were times when she almost gave up, she still refused to bow down to the temptations of Lucifer. She held fast to the promise of God—*"My grace is sufficient for you, for My strength is made perfect in weakness"* (2 Corinthians 12:9). Finally, her faithfulness and love for God began to bear fruit, and today she walks in victory. Both she and her husband are now financially secure, and they are the proud parents of a beautiful baby.

This young woman is a born-again believer who truly loves the Lord. Those from her past who approached her with things that did not "pertain to holiness and godliness" were shocked and amazed by her refusals. They didn't understand that the "old person" was no longer there. Old things had passed away and her life had became new. She had developed a personal relationship with Jesus, and she had discovered for herself who He really was and what He meant in her life, and she refused to turn away from Him.

Personal Relationship

Revelation knowledge can only come to those who have spent time building a relationship with God. In this kind of relationship, God can speak to you through His Word and reveal to you things you need to know about your personal life. This is when ignorance is defeated by knowledge. When the Word has been planted on the inside of you, it begins to blossom and reveal its beauty and life. But unless Jesus is revealed to you, you will only know *of* Him instead of actually *knowing* who He is and knowing Him *personally* and *intimately*.

Because I was reared in the Seventh Day Adventist Church and later converted to a Pentecostal denomination, I had heard a variety of teachings about what salvation supposedly is. And there were even times early in my ministry when I preached out of my intellect without the revelation truths of God. Yes, I was saved, but I lacked that intimate, personal relationship with God that I needed in order to reach people more effectively.

One night in the stillness of my bedroom—with no one there but God and me—I began to pray. Suddenly, there was a dramatic change, and I sensed that I was no longer praying but the Spirit of God was making intercession for me. Yes, God was baptizing me with the Holy Ghost! I was so charged as He spoke and revealed himself that I felt like I was on fire! And it was then that I began to understand the real meaning of who Christ really is—to me personally. He is not just a Bible character we learn about through theological knowledge, but He is the Messiah—He is Lord, and He is alive!

My Trip to Caesarea Philippi

Not long after my infilling of the Holy Spirit, the Lord carried me away in a series of dreams. In one of the dreams, He showed me a hot summer morning. I saw twelve men paddling a rather small boat toward a shore. As the dream unfolded, I saw a vision of Jesus and His disciples standing at Caesarea Philippi. I knew where I was in the dream because I knew Scripture quite well. This knowledge allowed me to follow Jesus and His disciples very closely, seeing for myself some of the events of Matthew, chapter 16.

As the scene at Philippi continued, I saw a large building that had been erected for the purpose of false teaching. The altars built inside were dripping with the blood of babies who had been sacrificed to Baal and other idols—offerings to gods made of wood, stone, and metal.

In that setting, Jesus turned to His disciples and said, *"Who do men say that I, the Son of Man, am?"* I watched and listened as eleven men related what others had to say about who He was. Eleven of these men offered no personal opinion, but Peter—who probably could have been voted "least likely to know"—came up with the right answer. He knew who Jesus was, and he proclaimed with a loud voice, "You are the Christ." Jesus, knowing that human kind had not yet received revelation about who He was, realized that Peter's knowledge could have only come from a personal relationship with God.

4

Keys To the Kingdom

"And I will give you the keys of the kingdom of heaven, and whatever you bind on earth will be bound in heaven, and whatever you loose on earth will be loosed in heaven" (Matthew 16:19).

Jesus not only recognized Peter for answering His question with preciseness, but He also gave him power to loose and to bind. He placed within the hands of Peter the keys of the kingdom. Peter was given the power to open doors that needed to be opened and to lock doors that needed to be shut. Keys give access, and anyone who holds the keys also holds within them a fair amount of power. However, Peter did not use this power for wicked or manipulative purposes. Instead, he reminded the elders that they should all feed the flock of God and be good examples.

The elders who are among you I exhort, I who am a fellow elder and a witness of the sufferings of Christ, and also a partaker of the glory that will be revealed: Shepherd the flock of God which is among you, serving as overseers, not by constraint but willingly, not for dishonest gain but eagerly; nor as being lords over those entrusted to you, but being examples to the flock (1 Peter 5:1-3).

In Acts 2:38-41, we see Peter exercising the power with authority and boldness. *Then Peter said to them, "Repent, and let every one of you be baptized in the name of Jesus Christ for the remission of sins; and you shall receive the gift of the Holy Spirit. For the promise is to you and to your children, and to all who are afar off, as many as the Lord our God will call." And with many other words he testified and exhorted them, saying, "Be saved from this perverse generation." Then those who gladly received his word were baptized; and that day about three thousand souls were added to them.*

Peter preached the Word of God and the benefits of repentance. The crowd received the Word, and as a result, about three thousand souls were saved. Indeed, he held the keys to destroy the rebellion against God, known as sin. And because he was not afraid to exercise this power, on that day, thousands were snatched from the darkness of hell and given the gift of eternal life.

After the death and resurrection of Jesus Christ, God sent His power to the Church in the person of the Holy Spirit. So although Jesus no longer walks the earth in the flesh, we can still take Him with us wherever we go. Jesus sent the Comforter—the Holy Spirit—to lead us, guide us, and to give us comfort and direction. Today, the Lord's Church is endowed with the power of God in their lives and has the revelation that the power of God is real, alive, and reigning.

Exercising the Authority of the Keys

For the weapons of our warfare are not carnal but mighty in God for pulling down strongholds (2 Corinthians 10:4).

Through God, we as Christians have the power to pull down the strongholds of hell. For God not only gave Peter authority from on high, but He left us with the same authority to defeat the trickery and deceitfulness of Satan.

God knew that without Him and His Holy Spirit dwelling on the inside of us, we were no match for the attacks of the enemy. So He provided the power and authority we need to come against the onslaught of the enemy. First John 4:4 says, *He who is in you is greater than he who is in the world.* We have the greater One residing in us, therefore, we need no natural means of warfare, for He has given us weapons much mightier than those of this world.

And with great power the apostles gave witness to the resurrection of the Lord Jesus. And great grace was upon them all (Acts 4:33).

The apostles were all filled with the Holy Ghost and testified of this resurrection with boldness and accuracy. Because of their great faith, none of them lacked anything, and upon hearing their testimonies, a great multitude believed.

Contrary to popular belief, God never intended for the Church to take a passive position. Instead, He wants His Church to be people of diligence and boldness.

"And from the days of John the Baptist until now the kingdom of heaven suffers violence, and the violent take it by force" (Matthew 11:12). Violence in this case is not a natural means of warfare, but is the boldness to stand for what the Word of God declares to be true. Sometimes this requires very unpopular decisions...and even confrontation. But it is comforting to know that the Lord intercedes on our behalf and that He lives on the

31

inside of us to guide and direct us in the way we should go.

Walk in Liberty

To know Christ is to fellowship with Him. If you truly desire to finally receive His direction and to walk in liberty and freedom from the bondage of traditionalism, simply submit to His Word, His will, and His way, knowing that He loves you and has a destiny for your life. *For I know the thoughts that I think toward you, says the Lord, thoughts of peace and not of evil, to give you a future and a hope* (Jeremiah 29:11).

Let today be the day that you boldly choose to let go of the past and walk in liberty, being led by the Spirit of God rather than by what others may tell you. Find out for yourself who Jesus is and what He has in store for your life.

Pray this prayer with me now:

Lord, I desire to be free from fear and the bonds of traditionalism. From this day forth, I choose to receive Your divine direction and will for my life. I repent for not seeking You earlier and for ignoring Your direction for my life until now. I pray that as I begin to fellowship with You more, I will truly gain knowledge and understanding of who You really are. In Christ's name I pray. Amen.